THE ILLUSTRATOR'S LIBRARY

Charcoal & Pastel

THE ILLUSTRATOR'S LIBRARY

Charcoal & Pastel

Franklin Watts
New York   London   Toronto   Sydney
1986

The authors would like to express their gratitude
to Frank Sloan, for his guidance and for his
enthusiastic commitment to their work.

Library of Congress Cataloging-in-Publication Data

Bolognese, Don.
Charcoal and pastel.

(The Illustrator's library)
Includes index.
Summary: Offers instructions in drawing with
charcoal and pastel, explaining the importance of
texture, line, motion, shapes, and patterns. Also
discusses various types of papers, crayons, chalks,
and other supplies.
1. Charcoal drawing—Technique—Juvenile literature.
2. Pastel drawing—Technique—Juvenile literature.
[1. Charcoal drawing—Technique. 2. Pastel drawing—
Technique. 3. Drawing—Technique] I. Raphael, Elaine.
II. Title. III. Series.
NC850.B65 1986   741.2   86-13286
ISBN 0-531-10226-2

C O N T E N T S

Hard and soft pastel on bristol board with highlights in white paint and white pastel pencil

Introduction

Have you noticed that some people tell a story very well? They seem to have a gift for choosing words. They know how to use language to capture and hold the attention of their listeners. Some people can do the same thing with pictures, and this form of storytelling is called illustration.

Storytelling is both ancient and honored. Most of the evidence of the past has come to us through words, songs, and pictures. The artists among the cave dwellers have left us a record of actual hunting scenes. The designers of ancient languages created picture symbols from everyday life. And a thousand years ago, when most people could not read, artists used the glorious colors of stained glass to tell stories from the Bible.

Today these examples of storytelling through pictures are considered great art. But in their own time these pictures were appreciated because they also provided information and entertainment. And today, with our advanced communications, the ability to tell a story well through illustration is more important than ever. The Illustrator's Library is designed to help you be the best storyteller you can be.

Alternate sketch for book cover; soft and hard pastels on tracing paper

C H A P T E R 1

Materials

Tens of thousands of years ago a prehistoric hunter took a stick of partially burned wood and with the charred end drew pictures of animals on the walls of a cave. Today, artists still use the same tool; we call it charcoal. And although today charcoal is manufactured and comes packaged in a variety of ways, it remains essentially the same medium that was used by the cave dweller.

Charcoal is an expressive medium; it lends itself to bold and dramatic drawing. But it can also be used to produce delicate tones. In the Renaissance it was the favored medium for doing studies for paintings. It was also the preferred tool for drawing the figure.

To add color and more tone to their drawings the Renaissance masters also used red and white chalk. These were often used on tinted papers. When pastels were developed several centuries ago, a whole new world of subtle shades and brilliant colors was added to the artist's tool kit. Then artists had a tool available to them that was both immediate and graphic in its effect. All of these tools have proved to be especially beneficial to the illustrator of today.

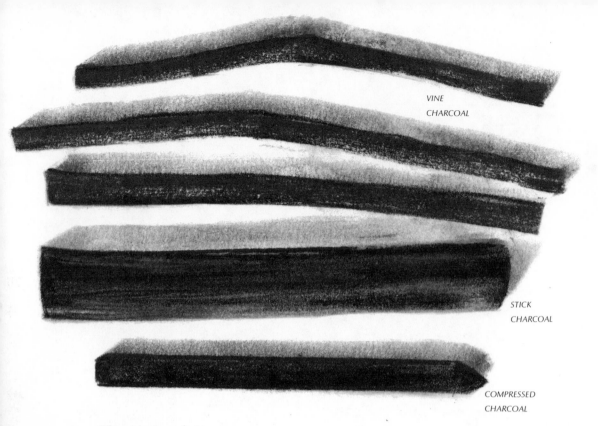

VINE
CHARCOAL

STICK
CHARCOAL

COMPRESSED
CHARCOAL

Charcoal

Charcoal comes in several forms and degrees of hardness. The result from using hard charcoal is usually less black than when you use soft charcoal. The finest grade of charcoal is made from vine twigs. These produce subtle tones but they are delicate and snap easily under pressure.

Compressed charcoal sticks are denser and more durable. Charcoal pencils, especially the harder ones (HB-B), are best for drawing lines and details. You can buy powdered charcoal; it is excellent for producing smoothly shaded tonal areas. You can also prepare powdered charcoal yourself by rubbing a charcoal stick on sandpaper.

Drawing done with charcoal and hard pastel on tracing paper

STUMP,
OR TORCHON

POWDERED CHARCOAL

*CHARCOAL AND
PASTEL PENCILS*

Pastels

Pastel comes from the word "paste" because that is exactly what pastel is—a paste of powdered pigment and gum.

Soft pastels are the most popular form of pastel. They are available in hundreds of brilliant shades and colors. If you've never used pastels before, get a starter set of about twelve colors. As your technique develops you will want to add specific colors. When you do, first check the makes, because the brands have slightly different shades. Select a light, medium, and dark tone of each color you choose. Also get several values of gray (some brands have neutral, warm, and cool grays).

HARD PASTELS

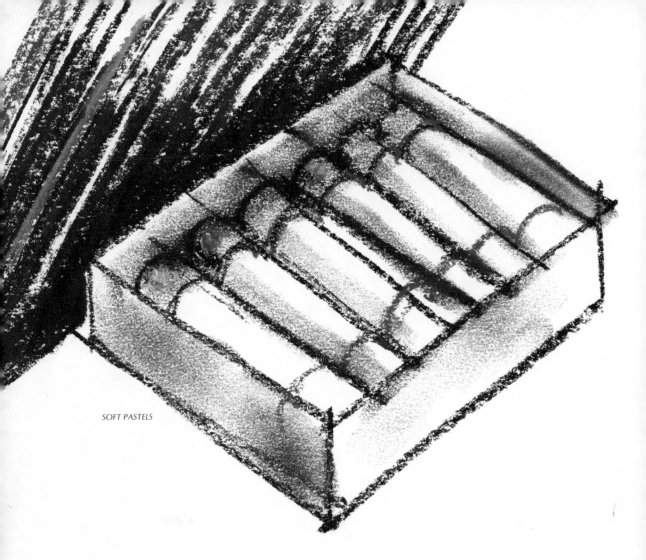

Hard pastels, though less brilliant than soft pastels, are stronger and better for linear work. They can be shaped to produce thin lines or used on their sides to create wide strokes. Hard and soft pastels work very well on textured charcoal paper, but hard pastels will also work well on paper with less texture, such as bristol board or vellum tracing.

Conté crayons are harder than hard pastels. They come in very few colors but they are an excellent drawing tool. Pastel pencils are good for adding detail and for touching up pastel drawings. Some artists use pastel pencils alone as an illustration medium.

SMALL TORCHONS

Drawing done in white and three gray shades of soft pastel and black hard pastel on two-ply medium text bristol

Erasers

Light charcoal strokes such as those made by vine sticks can be almost totally removed by wiping them with your hand or a clean cloth. If that doesn't work use a kneaded eraser. Don't rub with the eraser. Instead, press it firmly onto the area you want removed. Then lift the eraser. Twist the eraser to get a clean spot. Repeat the procedure. Do that several times to get rid of as much charcoal as possible before using a plastic or gum eraser to clean up the area.

You will need a good supply of kneaded erasers in charcoal work. You will use them not only as erasers but as drawing tools.

Torchons

Torchons are pointed rolls of paper that are used to rub and spread charcoal. Although rubbing with your finger does the job, torchons are sometimes more exact and cleaner. This is especially true when working with many colors. Small torchons are for detailed blending while large ones are best for broad areas.

ERASERS

Drawing done with charcoal, hard pastel, finger smudging, and kneaded eraser

Fixative

All charcoal and pastel drawings should be fixed or else the pigment will be rubbed off or will smudge. Fixative, however, must be used carefully, and most importantly, with adequate ventilation. Several light coats are better than one heavy coat. If fixative is sprayed too heavily and too closely to the artwork the drawing may become blurred.

Sharpeners and Sandpaper

Ordinary pencil sharpeners are useful only for the harder charcoal pencils and pastel pencils. Since the soft charcoal pencils (2B-6B) break easily they must be carefully sharpened with single-edge razor blades. Razor blades are also useful in shaping conté crayons and hard pastels. Vine or compressed charcoal sticks should only be shaped on a sandpaper block.

Other Supplies

White tempera paint is useful for highlighting. You will also need a few watercolor brushes—the small pointed variety.

Ask at your local art supply store for stencil alphabets. They can be used in the design of covers and posters. The stencils usually come in several styles and sizes—a 2½- or 3-inch- (6.35- or 7.62-cm-) high letter is a good start.

You should also have a few large spring clips for holding your paper to its support when you are sketching outdoors.

Masking tape is helpful in keeping the borders of your artwork clean.

Paper

The best way to learn about paper is to experiment with many different kinds. Papers made especially for charcoal and pastel come in white, black, several shades of gray, and tints of color. They all have textured surfaces. Most are available in either pads or single sheets.

A variety of tinted charcoal papers

Charcoal and pastel can also be used on ordinary sketching and newsprint pads, tracing paper (especially the heavier type called vellum), bristol board (only with a kid or vellum finish), and watercolor paper.

Charcoal and pastel pencils can be used on any paper suitable for an ordinary pencil (except for shiny or hot-pressed surfaces).

The Work Surface

Working with charcoal and pastel is messy and produces a lot of dust and particles. If you work on a tilted surface the dust may slide off your work. Some artists prefer working either at a standing easel or a smaller, desk-top folding easel. The smaller one is also handy for outdoor work.

Storage

You will quickly accumulate dozens of charcoal sticks, pastels, pencils, erasers, and so on. Use a separate surface or table (often called a taboret) to hold and store all your materials. A simple way to organize your loose pastels is to group them by color on a sheet of corrugated cardboard. Keep the delicate charcoal sticks in a box. And keep your unused paper clean. Put it in a drawer or a large envelope or store it in a simple portfolio.

C H A P T E R 2

Effects Through Texture

"Texture" is a word that is often associated with art. Actually texture is what we feel when we touch a substance. For example, even blindfolded you could probably identify a silk scarf or a woolen sweater merely by touching it. That's because each of those materials has a distinct texture.

If the scarf and the sweater were part of an illustration, the artist would have to create the effect of the two textures. The artist would be successful if a person looking at the picture could almost "feel" the silk and the wool. Since Nature provides so many textures, an illustrator must learn how to create effects that distinguish one texture from another. Developing these techniques is one big reason why illustrators experiment with different media. Charcoal and pastel are excellent for creating many of these textural effects.

Sandpaper scratched bristol board with charcoal pencil, highlighted with white pastel pencil

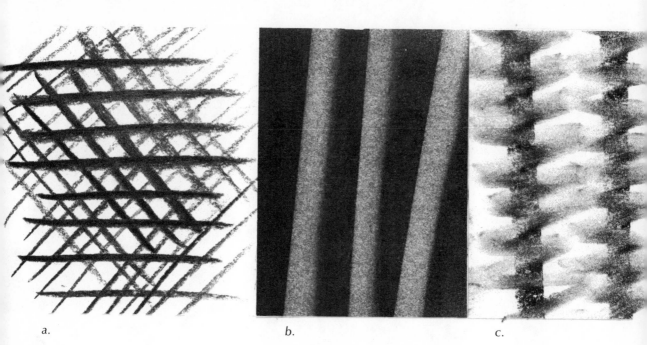

a.

b.

c.

a. charcoal stick—light pressure produces thin lines, heavier pressure thicker lines.
b. charcoal powder rubbed in, then erased with kneaded gum erasers
c. thick charcoal stick strokes rubbed with eraser
d. compressed charcoal stick lines—tones created by rubbing
e. soft pastel strokes
f. black and gray hard pastels—short eraser strokes
g. charcoal powder and charcoal pencil lines with white chalk for highlights

Art is full of surprises. These two pages of experimental texture drawings were done to demonstate specific techniques. However, they turned out to be something more.

Seen as a whole, these panels clearly illustrate the broad expressive possibilities of using charcoal. Compare the delicate line and subtle shading in the drawing of the lemon with the bold handling of charcoal in the fourth panel.

Look at the differences in line quality that can be achieved simply by adding pressure (Panel a). And would you have guessed that the dramatic lines on Panel b were made with only an eraser and rubbed charcoal?

Even the illustrator was surprised at the contrast in textures and the variety of effects that resulted from so few materials.

d.

e.

f.

g.

Here are two more examples of expressive illustration done
with the simplest of means. Both drawings share the same basic
composition and both use much the same materials. The man on
the left, however, was drawn on a textured paper. Using only
tones of charcoal and the surface texture of the paper, the artist
created a shadowy figure and an atmosphere of mystery. The

Black and gray hard pastels and charcoal pencil

drawing above, with its greater detail and definition, is suggestive of the main character in a story; this is a man with a story to tell.

Whatever their actual meanings, these two pictures demonstrate how a small change in approach and technique can produce a big difference in effect.

Different kinds of paper, from left to right: Black Strathmore; Light gray Canson; Medium gray Canson (less textured side)

Working with charcoal and pastel means experimenting with paper. And that means working on black as well as tinted sheets. Incidentally, brown wrapping paper is an excellent surface for charcoal and pastel. In addition to being inexpensive it also comes in very large sizes.

Try the following: get a large sheet of brown paper; tape it either to a wall or to the floor. Then do the largest drawing you

can imagine. Use a thick stick of charcoal and at least one or two light shades of pastel or chalk. One practical application of this experiment would be designs for the stage—maybe your school needs a set designer.

In any event, you will enjoy doing the large drawings—and working on a surface that is not white. Dark or tinted papers can make even a simple line drawing look more dramatic.

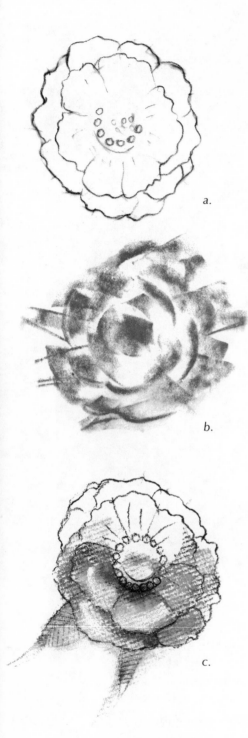

a.

b.

c.

The three illustrations on the left demonstrate a step-by-step method of combining textural strokes with linear detail. The first step is a simple line drawing (a). This is the "key" drawing, or guide. Although this one was done in charcoal pencil, a key drawing can be in any medium that produces a clear line. Put the key drawing on a lightbox. Then place a clean sheet of paper over it. With the side edge of a hard pastel, create the textured strokes following the pattern of the flower (b). The third illustration (c) is another version showing line details added over the textured strokes. Gray pastel has also been added. Illustrators frequently use key drawings as a way to experiment without losing the original drawing.

The illustration opposite shows the wide variety of textures that are possible with this medium.

Soft and hard pastels on smooth sketching paper, highlighted with white pastel

C H A P T E R 3

Line and Motion

As we saw in Chapter 2, charcoal is an excellent tool for creating textural effects. Charcoal offers another advantage to the illustrator: *immediacy.* Immediacy is from the word *immediate,* which means now! And that is all the time an illustrator has who is trying to record the action at a horse show, or a lion pacing back and forth at a zoo. For this kind of illustration an artist needs a tool that can be worked easily and quickly.

Charcoal is such a medium. With a few bold strokes an artist can freeze the motion of horse and rider. With a few well-placed smudges entire forms can be suggested.

And with a combination of line and tone entire compositions can be effectively and quickly captured. Of course, this is not as easy to accomplish as it looks.

Begin with observation and concentration and then practice. Visit places where you can observe action. It doesn't have to be a horse show or a zoo. It could be a gym or a neighborhood park or any place people are engaged in sports activities—where their attention is on what they are doing, not on your sketching.

Thin charcoal stick on sketch paper

Getting started is the hardest part. There is so much happening. What do you do first? Select one subject—for example, a horse and its rider. Watch them, but *don't* draw. Follow their every move. Look for something basic, like how the rider sits on the horse. Try to pick out a few simple lines that describe that action.

Then begin drawing. Use large strokes and don't worry about details. Draw a line from the horse's head to its tail; now draw the rider in one line, from the cap, down the back, all the way to the heel. These simple lines will establish the relationship between the horse and the rider. Practice these basic drawings again and again. After that the other parts of your live-action sketches will be much easier to do.

One suggestion that is often helpful: work big! Use a large pad and work with your whole arm, not just your hand and wrist. Charcoal is a terrific tool for doing large action sketches.

Drawings done with thin charcoal stick on sketch paper

Charcoal is also an excellent medium for adding tone to your quick figure studies. Try this by doing sketches of the riders as they wait or get ready. Use the same approach as before. Start by observing your model carefully. Study the posture, and note especially where the feet are in relation to the head and shoulders. Begin with line work. Then try adding, very quickly and roughly, large areas of tone—on the jacket, for instance. Don't be fussy and don't worry about mistakes. If you don't like your sketch, do another, and another.

Illustrators do a great many of these studies. Practice of this sort for an illustrator is like playing scales for a pianist.

Drawings done with thin and thick charcoal sticks on sketch paper

Charcoal stick on sketch paper

One of the rewards of looking at illustrations done in this medium and style is the feeling of "being there." This is another way of expressing what was said earlier about charcoal: it is a medium of *immediacy.*

Many illustrators use these sketches as a base for pastel color drawings. They are also an excellent reference source for future illustrations.

Opposite: charcoal stick on charcoal paper—tonal areas achieved by rubbing with a paper towel, highlights with kneaded eraser

Conté crayon and hard pastel are two drawing tools that are ideal for doing quick sketches. And one of the best places to practice is the zoo.

Do you know the expression: "More fun than a barrelful of monkeys"? That saying tells what we all feel when we watch monkeys at play. But watching is a lot easier than drawing. How do professional illustrators catch all that lively action? Some illustrators sketch from life, then refer to photos for details of form and color. Some even take along a camera when they go sketching and that is often the best solution. Of course you could start with an animal that doesn't move quite as fast as a monkey. One animal that comes to mind seems to have been designed just for charcoal drawings: the panda.

*Drawings done
with charcoal stick*

Compressed charcoal
stick on charcoal
paper

How could any artist pass up a chance to draw the majestic lion? You can draw the lion in two contrasting moods if you go just before feeding time. Then lions pace anxiously back and forth as they wait for their food. Right after it has been fed, a lion will relax and you'll have a better chance to work more slowly and to do more detailed drawings.

Drawings done with charcoal stick on sketch paper, kneaded eraser for highlights

C H A P T E R 4

Shapes and Patterns

The stylized illustration of Queen Elizabeth I on the opposite page reflects the formal and rigid style of dress that was typical during the 1600s. Unlike the soft fabrics and informal styles of today, "Elizabethan" clothing forced the figure to fit into basic geometric shapes. It is difficult to imagine a lady of the court running—or even sitting. However, from an artist's point of view, such costumes present a wonderful opportunity for the creation of stylized drawings and paintings.

In this chapter we will demonstrate how chalk and pastel can be used to produce geometric patterns. These simple shapes are often the inspiration for larger illustrations. You will also be introduced to the use of this medium for the drawing of volumes: simple geometric forms that appear to be three-dimensional.

Much of this work will be done on tinted paper (see Chapter 2), which lends itself very well to this use of chalk and pastel.

Charcoal pencil line drawing—hard and soft pastel worked in with torchon and fingers. Highlights with white pastel and white paint.

A circle, a triangle, and a rectangle are three simple shapes that are the design elements of the illustrations in this chapter. These geometric figures can be drawn in two basic styles: as two-dimensional shapes and as three-dimensional forms. Experimenting with both approaches is very easy with charcoal and pastel.

The illustrations on pages 40, 43, and 45 are examples of the two-dimensional, or decorative, approach. Begin by drawing these shapes in a loose and freehand manner. Use the ends of the pastel for the line work and the sides for large areas. Keep the drawings bold and direct.

Your experiments with variations of the basic geometric shapes will open up many new ways of working. For example, look closely at the illustration on page 40. The illustrator combined freehand drawing with stenciled designs based on the geometric shapes. Although the final result looks complicated, it isn't.

Gray hard pastels on vellum tracing paper

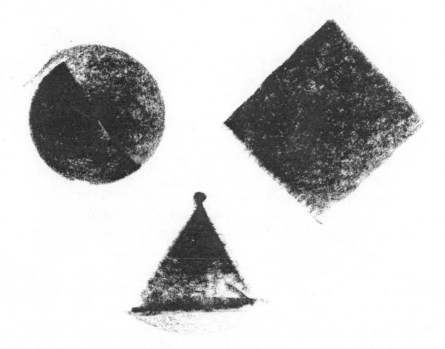

Opposite: line drawing with charcoal pencil edged with hard pastel and filled in with soft pastel

To begin, the artist did a simple tonal drawing (page 45). Then, using a straight edge, she ruled some lines with a charcoal pencil to create the diamond pattern on the dress. The circular and diamond-shaped patterns were created with a stencil.

The artist first drew the shapes on heavy vellum tracing paper. She then folded the paper and with a scissor cut out the pattern. She unfolded the stencil and placed it on the drawing. Holding the edges firmly to the paper, she rubbed pastel over the stencil area. This can be done either with your finger or a torchon. When you have finished the area, lift the stencil carefully.

Each layer of stenciled pattern must be fixed. That will permit you to change the color or tone of an area. However, when you put light pigment on top of a dark tone some of its brilliance will be lost when fixed. Some illustrators solve this by not spraying their final light tones. Another way of keeping highlights is dry-brushing (brushing with a minimum of water) white tempera over the light areas.

What about the other basic approach to geometric shapes? What will happen if you make the circle into a ball, the triangle into a cone or pyramid, and the rectangle into a box or cube? Now, the shapes appear to have three-dimensional form. By adding a little shading to some circles and putting them on a black background you create the illusion of space: an illustration of planets and moons.

Working with shaded geometric shapes opens the door to many illustration possibilities.

Both drawings: white, gray, and black pastels on black charcoal paper

The world of machines offers ideal opportunities. The old-fashioned steam locomotive is a perfect example. Its design is based on the same geometric forms that you have in front of you. The illustrator of the train poster on page 51 had the same idea, only he added one more element: stenciled lettering.

To test his idea he first did some small, or "thumbnail," sketches (above). The illustrator's next step was a larger version (page 49). He used a simple technique: hard pastel on vellum tracing paper. Tracing paper allows an artist to copy successful parts of earlier drawings. Charcoal on tracing paper is a quick and efficient technique for helping the illustrator develop his designs. In this case the artist decided to go ahead—with one big change. Since white and gray pastels work very well on dark paper, the final art would be done on black. The artist wanted the light tones to come out of the black background like a locomotive traveling through the night.

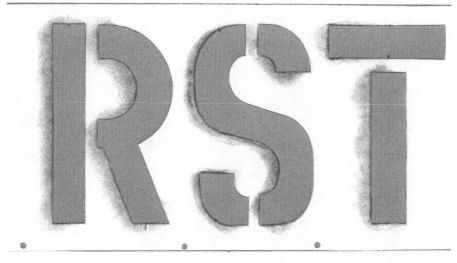

Actual stencil used

As part of his preparation the artist also tested the stenciled lettering on scraps of black paper. Satisfied that all the parts were going to work together, he completed the illustration using techniques that combined stenciling and freehand drawing. Templates were used to produce the circular forms. Pastel rubbed against straight edges of paper created the cowcatcher.

The geometric shapes used in this chapter are meant to be a starting point for design ideas. The same is true of the stencil technique. Work with them; experiment. You'll be surprised at how quickly you invent your own techniques.

Both drawings: white and gray pastels rubbed on black charcoal paper

CHAPTER 5

Book Covers

Have you ever wondered why most books have illustrations on their covers? A new book is like an unfamiliar brand of breakfast cereal—the contents are a complete mystery to you. An illustrated book cover is just like the front panel of a cereal box. It should give you a clue to the nature of what is inside, just as the illustration on the cereal box should let you know whether the cereal is flakes or shredded, with raisins or coated with sugar, or whatever.

The cover can't give you the whole story—or let you taste the flavor—but it should make you curious. And, most important, it should not be misleading. For example, take another look at the cover on this book. Then take a look at the drawing on page 8. This *was* the original design for the cover. But was it possible that someone, giving this drawing a quick glance, would *think* that the book would be about drawing faces?

The illustrators and the editor thought there was a possibility that people would be misled by the artwork, so they decided that only the materials should be pictured. The design was then changed to let the browser or reader *know* that the content of the book was about a specific technique of drawing.

This chapter will demonstrate the use of charcoal, chalk, and pastel in various combinations to create three book covers that represent areas of popular literature: ancient tales and myths, biography, and science fiction.

Charcoal pencils and kneaded eraser on vellum tracing paper

All sketches done with ordinary pencil and charcoal pencil and tracing paper

How does an illustrator begin designing a book cover? By reading the book if there is enough time. If there is not enough time, the publisher gives the artist a synopsis of the book with several suggestions or ideas for the cover design.

The artist then begins sketching ideas as clearly and quickly as possible. These sketches, though small, contain a lot of information that he or she may later want to elaborate in larger sketches. They also help the artist eliminate ideas that turn out not to be as good on paper as they were in the imagination.

The thumbnail phase ends when the artist has enough ideas to choose from. The next step is full-size sketches. This is when the artist refers to a picture collection: a file of magazine clippings, illustrated books, work by other artists, and the artist's own sketches and notebooks. This research time can be very rewarding. The solutions for both the Greek cover (page 52) and the robot cover (page 57, by the same artist) are from research the artist was doing on Greek warriors.

As the artist looked through pictures of armor he began getting ideas for robots. He realized that ancient warriors in suits of armor combined the two qualities that are often used to describe futuristic robots: human intelligence within a mechanical body. This understanding led to solutions for both covers. Nevertheless, the two covers are very different from each other.

For the Greek cover the artist emphasized the human element. He composed the picture as a close-up; the warrior's features are clearly visible. And the background suggests the natural world of sky and clouds. Charcoal pencil on vellum tracing paper allowed the artist to create subtle lines, decorative details, and a wide range of tones (highlighted with kneaded eraser).

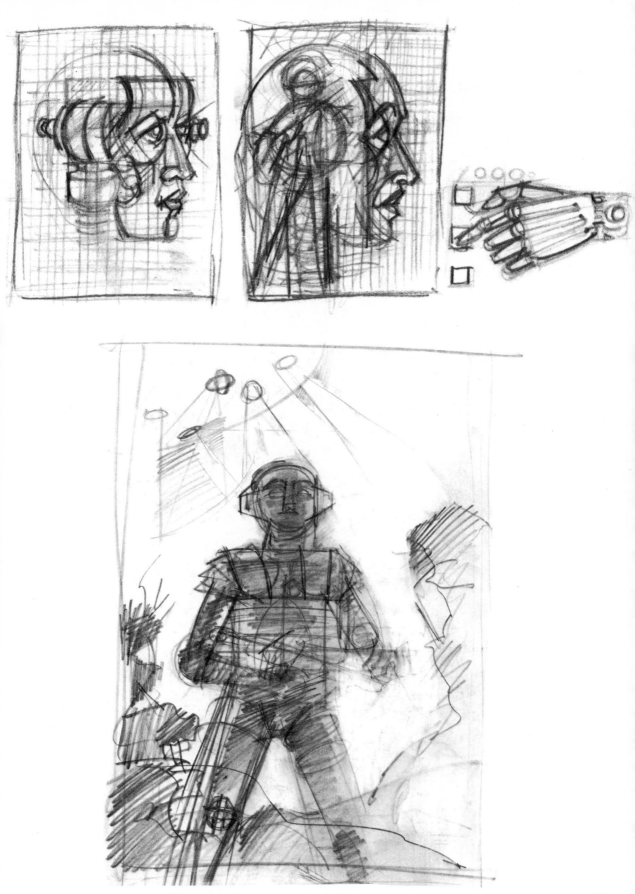

Hard pencil on vellum tracing paper

For the robot cover the artist stressed the opposite, the robot's nonhuman mechanical quality. He did this by putting the robot in an alien setting and silhouetting it with beams of light from a huge hovering spaceship. To heighten this effect he eliminated the line and detail work that was in the sketch above and used only rubbed black pastel. The artist believed this created an ominous and threatening cover—exactly the effect he was after. How would you have solved the problem? Would you have used a different approach, or another technique?

Opposite: powdered charcoal on bristol board

WAR OF THE ROBOTS

*Above: compressed char-
coal on charcoal paper;
right: compressed charcoal
on vellum tracing paper; far
right: charcoal and pastel on
tinted paper*

Good biographies of famous people are interesting and enter-
taining as well as informative. While telling us about a famous
person they also recreate the time period in which the person
lived.

Martin Luther King, Jr., was a famous person who lived during
a time of great social issues. How would an illustrator convey this
on a cover? Perhaps King should be shown at a rally, or leading a
march. Should King be portrayed in profile, full figure, sitting, or
standing? For help, the artist looked through dozens of books

and magazines with photos of the subject. The artist even listened to tapes of King's speeches.

Gradually King and the events surrounding him began to come to life in the artist's imagination. One image, in particular, began to dominate: King speaking, surrounded by supporters. The artist began sketching, trying to get an image on paper. At first he was concerned only with getting a good design, not with drawing an exact likeness of King. The sketches explored profiles, front views, three-quarter views, and different backgrounds.

Charcoal stick on charcoal paper

In all cases the artist kept King's face in close-up, for he felt this conveyed King's intensity and concern. The artist represented both the supporters and the drama of a social issue by a pattern of signs. The artist finally decided on the design. Howev-

White pastel on black charcoal paper

er, he still had two challenges to face. One was getting a likeness of King. The other was choosing an effective technique. To meet the first challenge the artist selected several photos of King that closely matched the cover design.

He then used ordinary lead pencils to draw a detailed likeness on tracing paper. This became the artist's working drawing, a reference for the finished illustration.

With that done the artist had to decide on a technique that conveyed the idea of a person speaking right at that moment. Charcoal—the perfect medium for on-the-spot drawing—was his choice. He added white and dark gray pastel for accents and shading on the tinted paper.

The basic drawing was done with bold strokes and the background was purposely left unfinished. As a final touch the artist designed the title to resemble quickly done signs.

These cover designs illustrate many different techniques for using charcoal and pastel. The surprising truth is that there are many more that you will discover through your own experiences.

Remember this important point: each medium has special qualities, such as the boldness of charcoal and the brilliance of pastel. Use them and experiment with them.

MARTIN LUTHER
KING JR

Index